READ, WRITE, AND PRACTICE

Look Inside
The Cow That Went OINK

Donna Alvermann
Connie A. Bridge
Barbara A. Schmidt
Lyndon W. Searfoss
Peter Winograd
Scott G. Paris

D.C. Heath and Company
HEATH Lexington, Massachusetts/Toronto, Ontario

Acknowledgments

Editorial **Director of Reading:** Tina Miller. **Managing Editor:** Kathleen T. Migdal. **Supervising Editor:** Susan D. Paro.
Editor: Jane M. Melick.
Production Coordinator: Bryan Quible.
Project Development: Brown Publishing Network, Inc.

Illustration 3-6: Renee Williams. **7-10:** Roseanne Litzinger. **11:** Valerie Spain. **12-13:** Cynthia Jabar. **14:** Andrea Barrett.
15-18: Rowen Barnes-Murphy. **19-21, 24:** Carolyn Croll. **22-23:** Susan Unger. **25:** Alex Walner. **26:** Melissa Sweet.
27-30: Mary Thelen. **31:** Andrea Barrett. **32:** Valerie Spain. **33-34:** Andrea Barrett. **35-38:** Diane Jaquith. **39:** Bari
Weissman. **40:** Bari Weissman. **41-42:** Cynthia Jabar. **43:** Melissa Sweet. **44:** Valerie Spain. **45-48:** James Marshall.
49: Bari Weissman. **50-51:** Carolyn Croll. **52:** Andrea Barrett. **53:** Cynthia Jabar. **54:** Valerie Spain. **55-58:** Benrei Huang.
59-62: Nick Catalano.

Published simultaneously in Canada
Printed in the United States of America
International Standard Book Number: 0-669-30215-5

7 8 9 10 – POO – 96 95

Name . . . .

airport

post office

school

zoo

hospital

supermarket

restaurant

house

Directions: Have children cut out the word/picture cards, and match them with the people cards on page 5.

Using vocabulary

Directions: Have children cut out the word/picture cards, and match them with place cards on page 3.

The Little House

They are all inside
the little house.
They are sleeping.

8

There is a little house.
It is red and white.
It is on Green Street.

2

Who is in here?
What are *they* doing?

7

Who is inside?
Look inside and see.

3

Who is in here?
What are they doing?

6

© D.C. Heath and Company

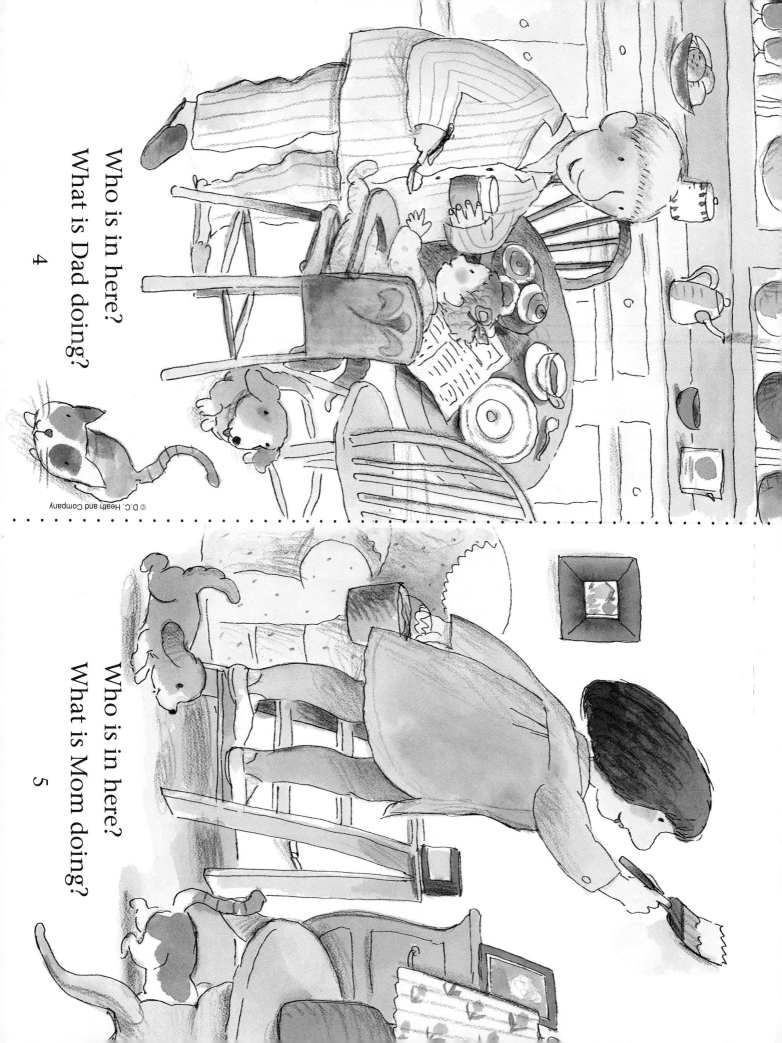

Who is in here?
What is Dad doing?

4

Who is in here?
What is Mom doing?

5

Name . . . .

a big bug

a little bug

inside the house

outside the house

a food I like

a food I hate

Directions: Have children draw pictures to illustrate the antonyms.

Understanding antonyms

Name . . . .

Tell about a zookeeper.

_____

- -

_____

- -

_____

_____

_____   _____

-    - - - - - - - -

_____

Tell about a supermarket.

_____

- -

_____

- .

_____   _____

_____   _____

- - - - - - - - - - - - - - - - - - -   - - - - - - - - - - -

_____   _____

Directions: Have children write sentences using the compound word given in the printed sentence. Below their sentence, children write the two small words in the compound word.

Using compound words

Name . . . .

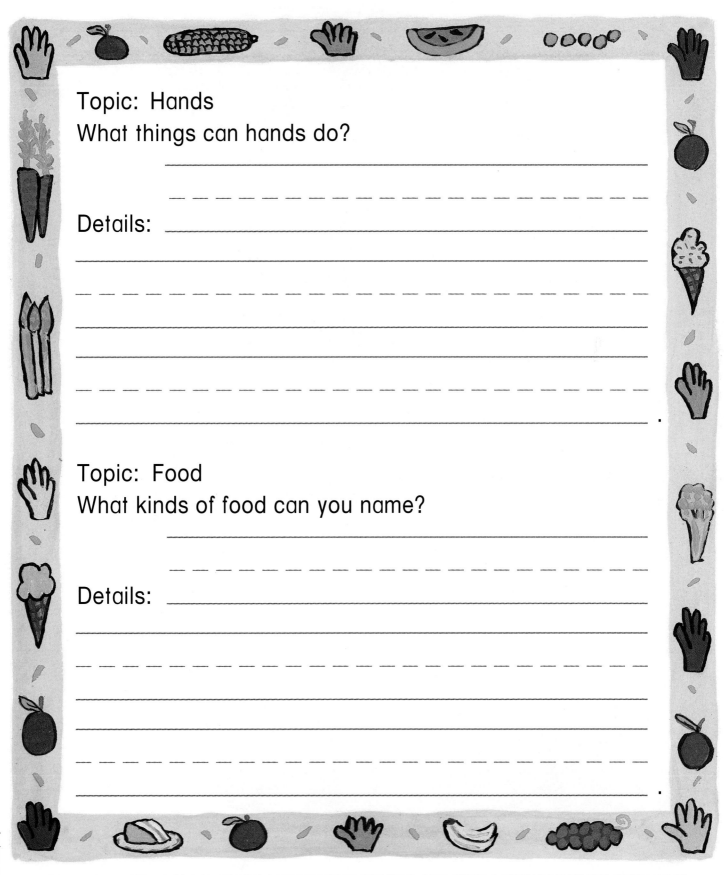

Topic: Hands
What things can hands do?

_____

— — — — — — — — — — — — — — — — —

Details: _____

_____

— — — — — — — — — — — — — — — — —

_____

— — — — — — — — — — — — — — — — —

_____ .

Topic: Food
What kinds of food can you name?

_____

— — — — — — — — — — — — — — — — —

Details: _____

_____

— — — — — — — — — — — — — — — — —

_____

_____

_____ .

Directions: Have children read each topic and question. Then have them write some details about what hands can do and about different kinds of food.

Writing details

Name ....

Directions: Have children cut out the shepherd. Then they will move the shepherd onto the words that begin with **sh** and **th** to help the shepherd find the path to his sheep. Children should also say the **sh** and **th** words as they go along.

Using consonant digraphs sh, th

Look Inside

The end

8

This is a fire house.
Look inside it.
Who can you see?

2

I see a bride and groom.
They are getting married.

7

I see a fire fighter.
He cleans the fire engine.

3

This is a church.
Look inside it.
Who can you see?

6

This is a bike shop.
Look inside it.
Who can you see?

4

I see a clerk.
She sells a bike.

5

Name . . . .

| clock | knife | lock | duck | sock | knobs | crack |

Directions: Have partners take turns reading a word and finding it in the picture. Then they draw lines from each word to the picture.

Using consonant digraphs kn, ck

Name ....

My Home

This is _____ .

It is _____ .

Look inside. You will see _____

_____ .

They _____

_____ .

Directions: Have children write an article about their own home or a house they would like to live in. Children can illustrate their article on another piece of paper.

20   LOOK INSIDE • Lesson 5   **Writing an article**

Name . . . .

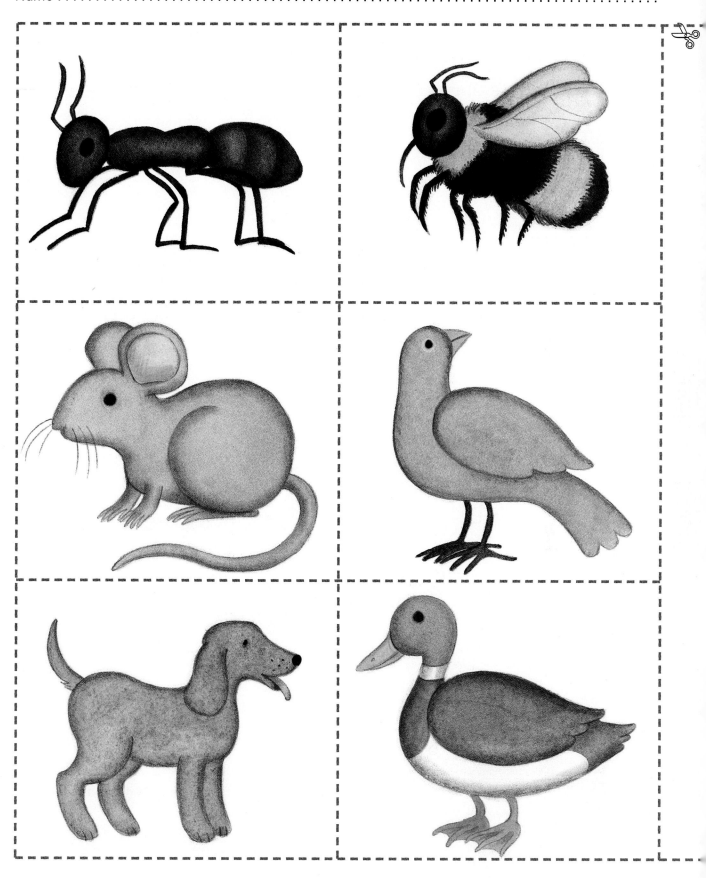

Directions: Have children cut along the dotted lines to cut apart the pictures to make animal cards. Children can use these cards to match with the animal home cards on page 24.

Name . . . .

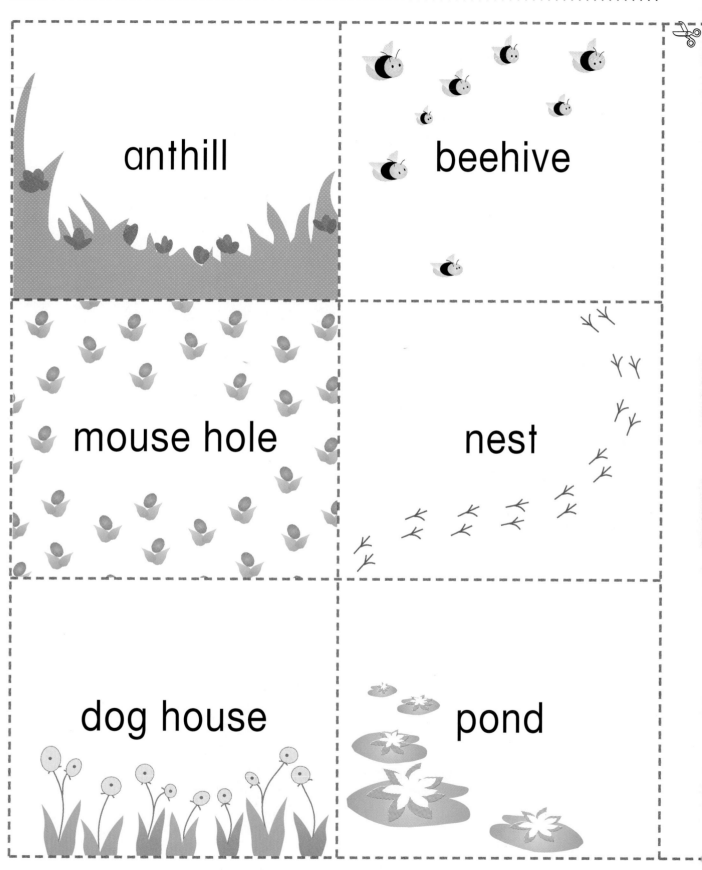

anthill

beehive

mouse hole

nest

dog house

pond

Directions: Have children cut out the word/picture cards. The words above can be used to read names of animal homes, to practice reading compound words, and to match with the animal cards on page 21.

LOOK INSIDE • Science Center

Name ....

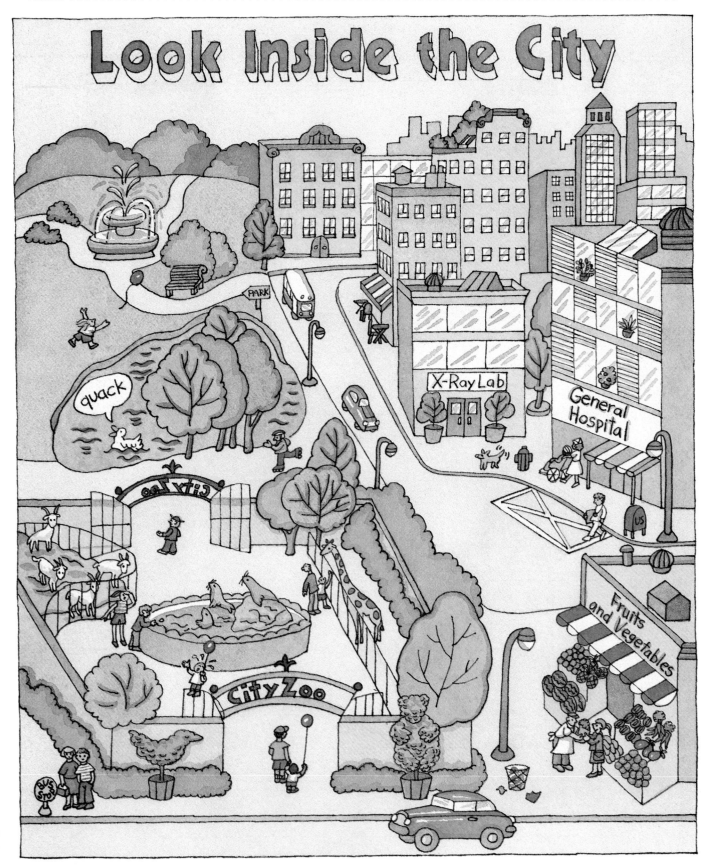

Directions: Have children work with a partner to tell each other what they see. They might use a separate sheet of paper to list their answers and compare answers with the rest of the group.

Using initial consonants q, v, x, z, c **(circle)**, g **(giant)**

Name ....

_____

- -

_____

- -

_____

- -

_____

- -

_____

Directions: Have children talk about the pictures. Then have them predict what they think the boy will do next and write what they think will happen. When finished, children can share what they've written with a friend.

Predicting outcomes

Hats off!

He puts mail in the mailbox.

Hats off to all these people!

8

This is the city.
You can see people.
You can see their hats!

2

Whose hat is this?

7

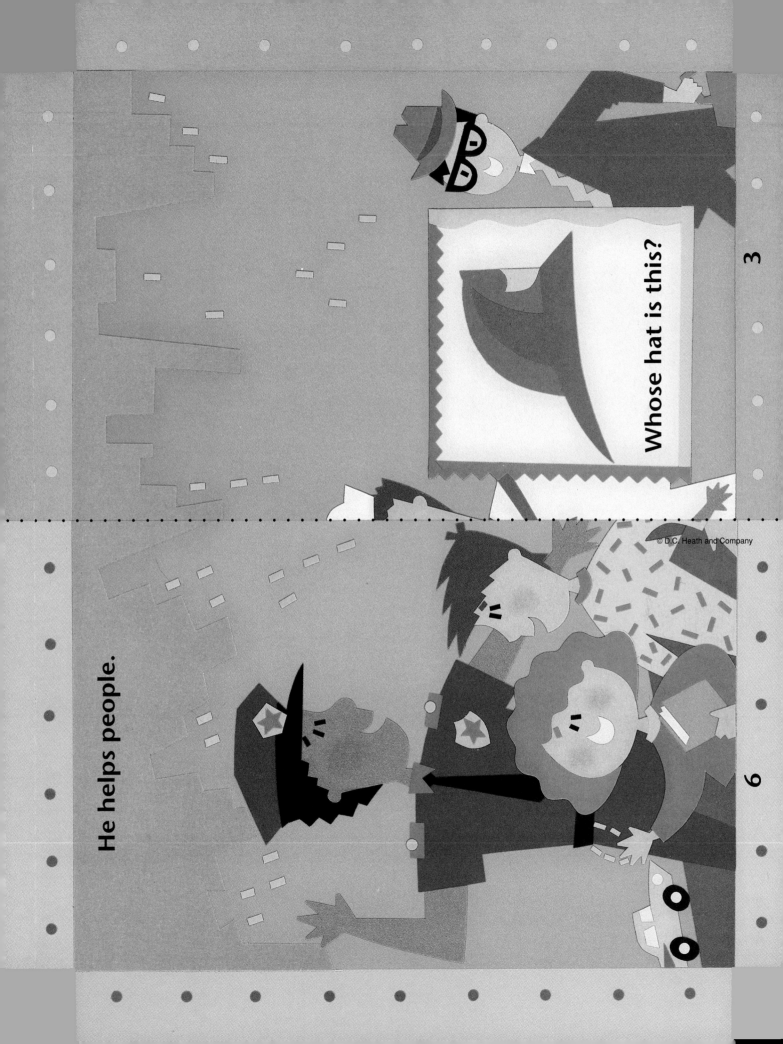

Whose hat is this?

3

He helps people.

6

She puts out fires.

Whose hat is this?

4

5

Name...

Write About the Picture

_____

- -

_____

- -

_____.

_____

- -

_____

- -

_____.

Directions: Have children write a sentence about each picture. Children should use the word **cooks** in the first sentence and **feeds** in the second sentence.

Using inflections: (verb -s)

Name . . . .

What I'd Like to Be

When I grow up, I want to be

_____

- -

_____ .

_____

- -

I will _____

_____

- -

_____

_____

- -

_____ .

Directions: Have children write about what they want to be when they grow up by completing each sentence — the first sentence with a word telling what they will be, the second with a description of what they will do in that job. Children can use the space below their writing to illustrate it.

Writing about what I'd like to be

Directions: Have the children cut out the picture and word cards. Then have them match each animal to its sound. These cards may also be used to play "Go Fish" or "Concentration."

Chick waited and waited.
And he did get his wish!

8

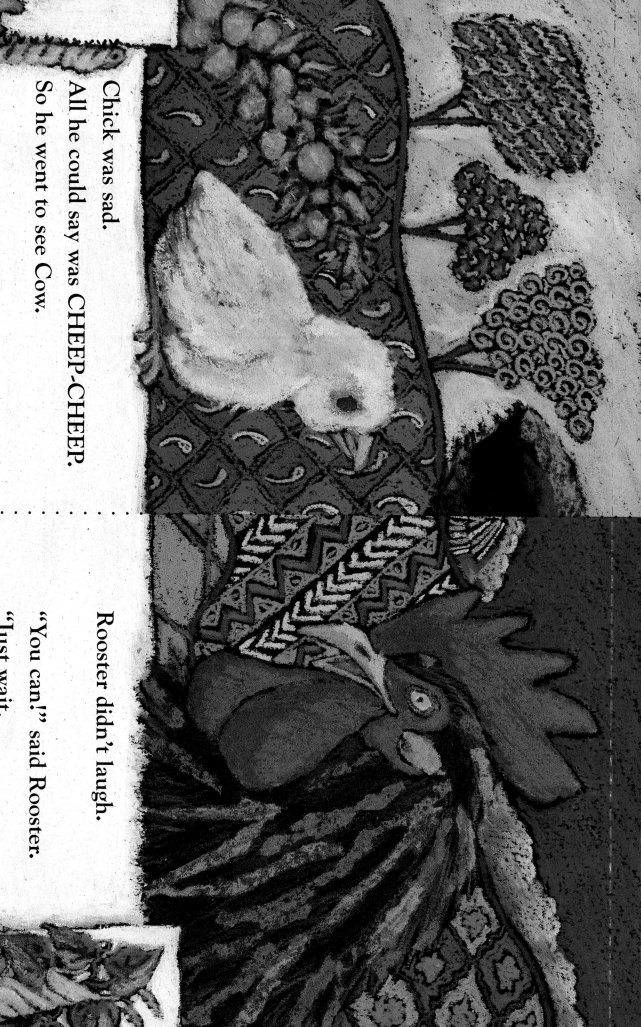

Chick was sad.
All he could say was CHEEP-CHEEP.
So he went to see Cow.
Chick said to Cow,
"I wish I could say MOO."

Rooster didn't laugh.
"You can!" said Rooster.
"Just wait.
You will get your wish."

Cow laughed and laughed.

Cow said to Chick,
"You cannot say MOO.
But you can say CHEEP-CHEEP."

3

Now Chick was very sad.
He went to see Rooster.

Chick said to Rooster,
"I wish I could say
COCK-A-DOODLE-DOO."

6

Chick was sad.
He went to see Duck.

Chick said to Duck,
"I wish I could say QUACK."

4

Duck laughed and laughed.

Duck said to Chick,
"You cannot say QUACK.
But you can say CHEEP-CHEEP."

5

Name ....

Directions: Have children cut out the story characters and use them to retell the story.

Retelling a story

THE COW THAT WENT OINK • Lesson 2

Name . . . .

This cow is sad.

This cow is happy.

This pig is big.

This pig is little.

This cat is inside a box.

This cat is outside a box.

Directions: Have children draw a picture in each box to illustrate the sentence.

Understanding antonyms

Name . . . .

Pig Made a Wish

Pig was sad. _____

_ _

Pig said, "I wish I could _____

_____

_ _

_____

_____ "

_ _

_____ .

Directions: Have children finish the story by writing about what Pig wished—something that would make Pig happy! Then children can illustrate their story.

THE COW THAT WENT OINK • Lesson 3

Writing

Name . . . .

I am very sleepy because

_____

_____

_____

_____ .

I am very happy because

_____

_____

_____

_____ .

I am very mad because

_____

_____

_____

_____ .

Directions: Children look at the picture and then finish the sentence telling why it happened.

Name . . . .

This puppy is very hungry!

This puppy is happy.

This puppy has a black body.

This puppy has a funny hat.

This puppy ate some jelly.

Directions: Have children read each sentence and then illustrate it.

Reading words with the long vowel y

The Funny Fox

"I made that cake for you," said Mom.

"That is not funny!" said the fox. "That is not funny at all!"

8

The Funny Fox

"I am a funny fox,"
said the fox.
"Now I will do some
very funny things."

2

"Look out! Here I come!"
said the fox.

"Help!" said Mom.

7

"Look out! Here I come!"
said the fox.

"Help!" said the cat.

3

"That is not funny!"
said the dog.

"I think it is very funny,"
said the fox.

6

"This is not funny!"
said the cat.

"I think it is very funny,"
said the fox.

4

"Look out! Here I come!"
said the fox.

"Help!" said the dog.

5

Name . . . .

_____

- - - - - - - - - - - - - - -

_____

a surprise!

wh

The cow went OINK
_____

- - - - - - - - - - - - - - -

_____

the pig went MOO.

I will
_____

- - - - - - - - - - - - - - -

_____

you.

ch

_____

- - - - - - - - - - - - - - -

_____

of them could MOO and OINK.

Directions: Children find two words from the story that begin with **wh** (what, while) and write them in the correct speech balloons. Then children find two words from the story that end with **ch** (each, teach) and write them in the correct speech balloons.

Writing words with consonant digraphs ch,wh

Name . . . .

Directions: Have children draw a picture of the two main characters in the story setting.

THE COW THAT WENT OINK • Lesson 5

Understanding story elements (character, setting)

Name . . . .

Directions: Have children write about what happened in the story.

Understanding story elements (plot)   THE COW THAT WENT OINK • Lesson 5   51

Name . . . .

Two Farm Animals

_____   _____

The _____ can say _____ .

_____   _____

The _____ can say _____ .

They teach each other.

                                        _____

Now each of them can say _____

_____

_____ .

Directions: Have children complete each sentence with an animal's name and its sound, and the last sentence with both sounds. Children can illustrate their story with a picture of the two animals and speech balloons here or on another piece of paper.

Writing a story about animal sounds

Name . . . .

This pig rolled in mud.

This pig _____

_ _ _ _ _ _ _ _ _ _ _ _

This pig _____

did not

roll in the mud.

The fox is in the bushes.

_____

_ _ _ _ _ _ _ _ _ _ _ _

The fox _____

is not

in the bushes.

Directions: Children read the first sentence and look at the picture. Then they read the second sentence, fill in the contraction, and draw a picture to tell about the sentence.

Using contractions

Name . . . .

My favorite animal is the _____.

_____

_____

I like this animal because _____

_____

_____

_____

_____ .

Directions: Have children write the name of their favorite story character and tell why they like than animal best. Then children can illustrate their writing by drawing that animal.

Writing about a favorite animal

Where Is Baby Pig?

"Oh, there you are!"
said Mother Pig.

Now she will teach Baby Pig
not to go too far.

8

"Where is Baby Pig?"
asked Mother Pig.
"Where, oh where, can
that little pig be?"

2

Mother Pig looked and looked again.
"I will look inside
that house," she said.

7

Mother Pig looked and looked.
She looked here.
She looked there.
She looked everywhere!

3

"Do you know where Baby Pig is?"
asked Mother Pig.

"No," said the turkey.
"Baby Pig isn't here."

6

"Do you know where Baby Pig is?" asked Mother Pig.

"No," said the sheep.
"Baby Pig isn't here."

4

"Do you know where Baby Pig is?" asked Mother Pig.

"No," said the donkey.
"Baby Pig isn't here."

5

8

Farmer Brown saw a bee.
She said, "Oh, oh!
Watch out!
It's a bee!"

2

"Buzz, buzz," said the bee.
"You'll see!"

7

"Buzz, buzz" said the bee.
"Come with me!"

3

"Why are we going there?"
asked Farmer Brown.

6

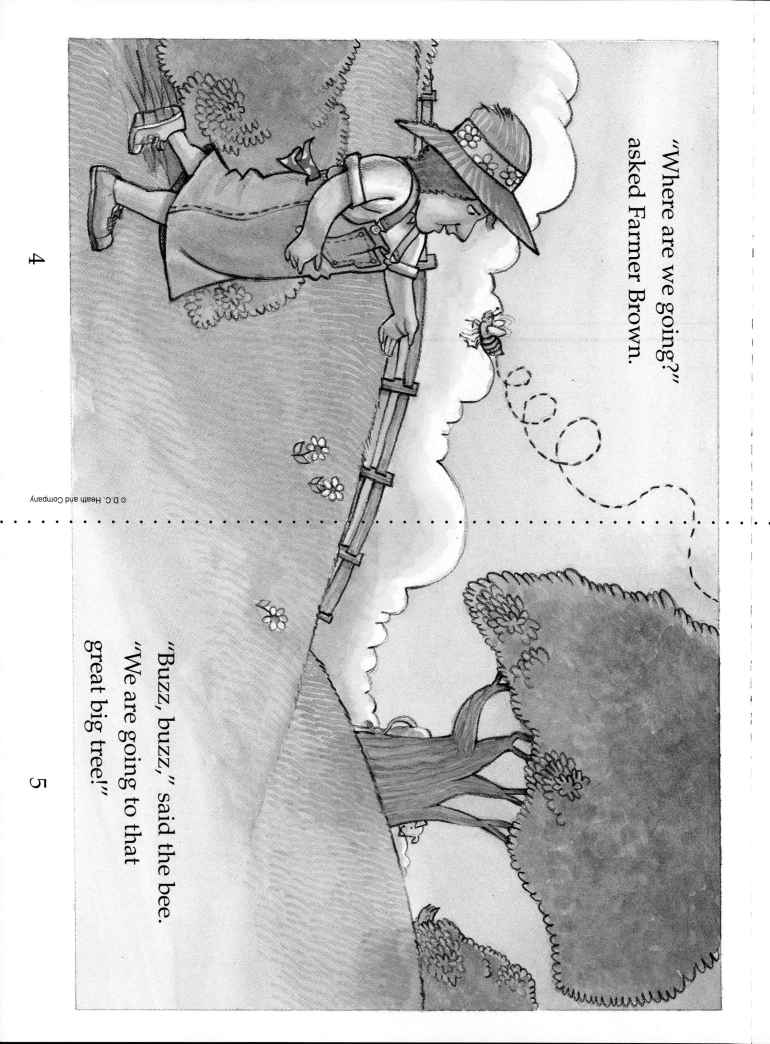

"Where are we going?"
asked Farmer Brown.

4

"Buzz, buzz," said the bee.
"We are going to that
great big tree!"

5

Name . . . .

I can read.

Directions: Have the children cut out, color, and decorate their certificate of achievement.